The meaning of a word
— to me — is not as exact
as the meaning of a color.
Colors and shapes
make a more definite
statement than words.

Georgia O'Keeffe, 1976

GEORGIA O'KEEFFE

WORDS | WORKS

VOLUME ONE

GEORGIA O'KEEFFE MUSEUM
SANTA FE, NEW MEXICO

I want real things — live people to take hold of
— to see — and talk to —
Music that makes holes in the sky —

Letter to Anita Pollitzer, 1916

Sunrise and Little Clouds No. II, 1916

I realized that I had things in my head not like
what I had been taught — not like what I had seen
— shapes and ideas so familiar to me that
it hadn't occurred to me to put them down.
I decided to stop painting, to put away
everything I had done, and to start
to say the things that were my own.
This was one of the best times in my life.
There was no one around to look at
what I was doing — no one interested
— no one to say anything about it
one way or another. I was alone and
singularly free, working into my own,
unknown — no one to satisfy but myself.

Some Memories of Drawings, 1974

Black Lines, 1916

Abstraction White Rose, 1927

I feel that a real living form is the natural result
of the individual's effort to create the living thing
out of the adventure of his spirit into the unknown
— where it has experienced something — felt something —
it has not understood — and from that experience
comes the desire to make the unknown — known —

Making the unknown — known — in terms of one's medium
is all absorbing — if you stop to think of form — as form
you are lost — The artist's form must be inevitable —
You mustn't think you won't succeed —

Letter to Sherwood Anderson, 1923

Alfred Stieglitz, *Georgia O'Keeffe – Hands*, 1919

I had this desire and interest in painting
to want to do my own things.

Statement in *New York World-Telegram*, 1945

I walked out past the last house — past the last locust tree —
and sat on the fence for a long time — looking — just looking at
— the lightning — you see there was nothing but sky and
flat prairie land — land that seems more like the ocean than
anything else I know — There was a wonderful moon.

Letter to Anita Pollitzer, 1916

Evening Star No. VI, 1917

I am loving the plains more than ever it seems — and the SKY —
… you have never seen SKY — it is wonderful —

Letter to Anita Pollitzer, 1916

Color is one of the great things in the world
that makes life worth living to me
and as I have come to think of painting
it is my effort to create an equivalent
with paint color for the world — life as I see it.

Letter to William M. Milliken, 1930

— It is something I wanted very much to tell someone —
and what I wanted to express was a feeling like
wonderful music gives me —

Letter to Anita Pollitzer, 1915

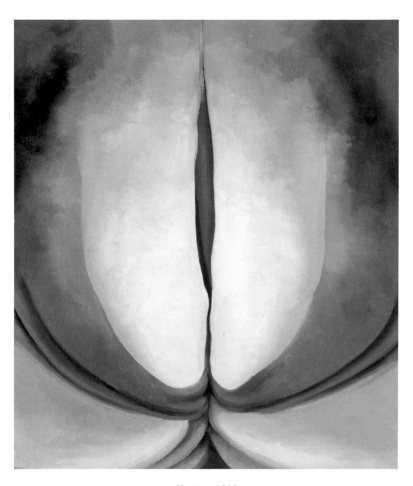

Blue Line, 1919

Black Hollyhock Blue Larkspur, 1930

Everyone has many associations with a flower —
the idea of flowers. You put out your hand to touch
the flower — lean forward to smell it — maybe
touch it with your lips almost without thinking —
or give it to someone to please them.
Still — in a way — nobody sees a flower —
really — it is so small . . .

So I said to myself — I'll paint what I see —
what the flower is to me but I'll paint it big and
they will be surprised into taking time to look at it —
I will make even busy New Yorkers take time
to see what I see of flowers.

Statement in *An American Place* Exhibition Catalogue, 1939

For me, painting the crosses was
a way of painting the country.

Georgia O'Keeffe, 1976

Cross with Red Sky, 1929

My Front Yard, Summer, 1941

It's the most wonderful place you can imagine.
It's so beautiful there. It's ridiculous.
In front of my house there are low scrub bushes
and cottonwood trees and, further out,
a line of hills. And then I have this mountain.
A flat top mountain that slopes off on each side.
A blue mountain. And to the left you can see
snow covered mountains, far, far away.

Statement in *New York World-Telegram*, 1945

Give my greetings to the sky and the mountains
and the sun and the wind.

Letter to Dorothy Brett, 1932

Mule's Skull with Pink Poinsettia, 1936

Tell me what you think Art is — if you can
— ask a lot of people — and see if anybody knows . . .
You asked me about music — I like it better than anything
in the world — Color gives me the same thrill once in
a long long time — I can almost remember and count the times
— it is usually just the outdoors or the flowers — or a person —
sometimes a story — or something that will call a picture
to my mind — will affect me like music —

Letter to Anita Pollitzer, 1915

Untitled (Red and Yellow Cliffs), 1940

We have been having perfect days of perfect quiet sunshine — working lots — and I feel like singing.

Letter to Sherwood Anderson, 1923

The only reason I don't want to die is because I would never see this country again.

Statement in *House and Garden*, 1965

If you can believe in what you are and keep to your line
— that is the most one can do with life.

Letter to Maria Chabot, 1944

Ram's Head, Blue Morning Glory, 1938

Maria Chabot, *Georgia O'Keeffe Hitching a Ride to Abiquiu with Maurice Grosser*, 1944

I believe in women making their own living.
It will be nice when women have equal opportunities
and status with men so that it is taken as a matter of
course. I think there are some men who would like
to cook and keep house. Why shouldn't they?

Statement in *New York World-Telegram*, 1945

In the Patio VIII, 1950

That door is what made me buy this house.
I waited ten years to get the house, because of that door.

Statement in *ArtNews*, 1977

Don't think that I really underrate my way of thinking
— or moving into the world — or whatever you want to call it
— It is just my way of being — and I just have wits enough
to know that if you really sift to the bottom any more
reasonable approach to life or any particular problem
— it really isn't any more rational than mine is.

Letter to Waldo Frank, 1926

The world all simplified and beautiful and clear-cut
in patterns like time and history will simplify and
straighten out these times of ours — What one sees
from the air is so simple and so beautiful I cannot
help feeling that it would do something wonderful
for the human race —

Letter to Maria Chabot, 1941

Above the Clouds I, 1962/1963

. . . I like the artist standing up for himself
— believing in his own word no matter
what anyone may say about it.

Letter to Cady Wells, 1938

Blue Black and Grey, 1960

Tony Vaccaro, *O'Keeffe at the Ranch*, 1960

Where I was born and where and
how I have lived is unimportant.
It is what I have done with where I
have been that should be of interest.

Georgia O'Keeffe, 1976

CREDITS

Front Cover: Alfred Stieglitz
Georgia O'Keeffe, 1918
Palladium print
Gift of The Georgia O'Keeffe Foundation
2003.01.002/AS 474

Page 1: Georgia O'Keeffe, *Georgia O'Keeffe*, p. 1. New York: Viking Press, 1976. © Juan Hamilton

Page 2: Georgia O'Keeffe *Jimson Weed*, 1932
Oil on canvas
Gift of The Burnett Foundation
1996.01.001/CR# 815

Page 4: Clive Giboire, ed., *Lovingly, Georgia: The Complete Correspondence of Georgia O'Keeffe and Anita Pollitzer*, p. 123. To Anita Pollitzer, January 14, 1916, Columbia, SC. New York: Simon and Schuster, 1990.

Page 5: Georgia O'Keeffe *Sunrise and Little Clouds No. II*, 1916, watercolor on paper
Gift of The Burnett Foundation
1997.18.01/CR# 134

Page 6: Georgia O'Keeffe, *Some Memories of Drawings*, ed. Doris Bry, p. 7. New York: Atlantis Editions, 1974.

Page 7: Georgia O'Keeffe *Black Lines*, 1916
Watercolor on paper
Gift of The Burnett Foundation
2007.01.001/CR# 63

Page 8: Georgia O'Keeffe *Abstraction White Rose*, 1927
Oil on canvas
Gift of The Burnett Foundation and The Georgia O'Keeffe Foundation
1997.04.002/CR# 599

Page 9: Jack Cowart and Juan Hamilton, letters selected and annotated by Sarah Greenough, *Georgia O'Keeffe: Art and Letters*, p. 174. To Sherwood Anderson, September 1923,* Lake George. Washington, DC: National Gallery of Art in association with New York Graphic Society Books, 1987.

Page 10: Alfred Stieglitz *Georgia O'Keeffe – Hands*, 1919, palladium print
Gift of The Georgia O'Keeffe Foundation
2003.01.003/AS 567

Page 11: Carol Taylor, "Lady Dynamo: Miss O'Keeffe, Noted Artist, Is a Feminist," *New York World-Telegram* (March 31, 1945), sec. 2, p. 9.

Page 12: Clive Giboire, ed., *Lovingly, Georgia: The Complete Correspondence of Georgia O'Keeffe and Anita Pollitzer*, p. 183. To Anita Pollitzer, September 11, 1916, Canyon, TX. New York: Simon and Schuster, 1990.

Page 13: Georgia O'Keeffe *Evening Star No. VI*, 1917
Watercolor on paper
Gift of The Burnett Foundation
1997.18.003/CR# 204

Clive Giboire, ed., *Lovingly, Georgia: The Complete Correspondence of Georgia O'Keeffe and Anita Pollitzer*, p. 184. To Anita Pollitzer, September 11, 1916, Canyon, TX. New York: Simon and Schuster, 1990.

Page 15: Jack Cowart and Juan Hamilton, letters selected and annotated by Sarah Greenough, *Georgia O'Keeffe: Art and Letters*, p. 202. To William M. Milliken, November 1, 1930, The

Shelton Hotel, New York. Washington, DC: National Gallery of Art in association with New York Graphic Society Books, 1987.

Page 16: Clive Giboire, ed., *Lovingly, Georgia: The Complete Correspondence of Georgia O'Keeffe and Anita Pollitzer*, p. 5. To Anita Pollitzer, June 1915, Charlottesville, VA. New York: Simon and Schuster, 1990.

Page 17: Georgia O'Keeffe *Blue Line*, 1919 Oil on canvas Gift of The Burnett Foundation and The Georgia O'Keeffe Foundation 1997.04.004/CR# 294

Page 18: Georgia O'Keeffe *Black Hollyhock Blue Larkspur*, 1930, oil on canvas Extended Loan, Private Collection 1997.03.001/CR# 714

Page 19: Georgia O'Keeffe, *Georgia O'Keeffe: Exhibition of Oils and Pastels*, p. 2. New York: An American Place, January 22–March 17, 1939.

Page 20: Georgia O'Keeffe, *Georgia O'Keeffe*, p. 122, plate 64. New York: Viking Press, 1976. © Juan Hamilton

Page 21: Georgia O'Keeffe *Cross with Red Sky*, 1929 Oil on canvas Copyright 2013 Courtesy the Gerald Peters Gallery, Santa Fe, New Mexico CR# 669

Page 22: Georgia O'Keeffe *My Front Yard, Summer*, 1941 Oil on canvas Gift of The Georgia O'Keeffe Foundation 2006.05.173/CR# 1023

Page 23: Carol Taylor, "Lady Dynamo: Miss O'Keeffe, Noted Artist, Is a Feminist," *New York World-Telegram* (March 31, 1945), sec. 2, p. 9.

Page 24: Jack Cowart and Juan Hamilton, letters selected and annotated by Sarah Greenough, *Georgia O'Keeffe: Art and Letters*, p. 206. To Dorothy Brett, mid-February 1932, New York. Washington, DC: National Gallery of Art in association with New York Graphic Society Books, 1987.

Page 25: Georgia O'Keeffe *Mule's Skull with Pink Poinsettia*, 1936 Oil on canvas Georgia O'Keeffe Museum Gift of The Burnett Foundation 1997.06.014/CR# 876

Page 27: Jack Cowart and Juan Hamilton, letters selected and annotated by Sarah Greenough, *Georgia O'Keeffe: Art and Letters*, p. 146. To Anita Pollitzer, October 20, 1915,* Columbia, SC. Washington, DC: National Gallery of Art in association with New York Graphic Society Books, 1987.

Page 28: Georgia O'Keeffe *Untitled (Red and Yellow Cliffs)*, 1940, oil on canvas Gift of The Burnett Foundation 1997.06.036/CR# 998

Jack Cowart and Juan Hamilton, letters selected and annotated by Sarah Greenough, *Georgia O'Keeffe: Art and Letters*, p. 173. To Sherwood Anderson, September 1923,* Lake George. Washington, DC: National Gallery of Art in association with New York Graphic Society Books, 1987.

Page 29: "Five Famous Artists in Their Personal Backgrounds," *House and Garden* vol. 126, no. 6 (December 1965), p. 176.

Page 30: Barbara Buhler Lynes and Ann Paden, eds., *Maria Chabot – Georgia O'Keeffe: Correspondence*

1941–1949, p. 160.
To Maria Chabot, January
19, 1944, New York.
Albuquerque: University
of New Mexico Press;
Santa Fe: Georgia O'Keeffe
Museum, 2003.

Page 31: Georgia O'Keeffe
*Ram's Head, Blue Morning
Glory*, 1938, oil on canvas
Gift of The Burnett Foundation
2007.01.024/CR# 940

Page 32: Maria Chabot
*Georgia O'Keeffe Hitching
a Ride to Abiquiu with
Maurice Grosser*, 1944
Photographic print
Gift of Maria Chabot
RC-2001-002-140

Page 33: Carol Taylor,
"Lady Dynamo: Miss O'Keeffe,
Noted Artist, Is a Feminist,"
New York World-Telegram
(March 31, 1945),
sec. 2, p. 9.

Page 34: Georgia O'Keeffe
In the Patio VIII, 1950
Oil on canvas
Gift of The Burnett Foundation
and The Georgia O'Keeffe
Foundation
1997.05.008/CR# 1211

Page 35: Mary Lynn Kotz,
"Georgia O'Keeffe at 90:
'Filling a Space in a Beautiful

Way. That's What Art Means to
Me'," *ArtNews* vol. 76, no. 10
(December 1977), p. 37.

Page 37: Jack Cowart and
Juan Hamilton, letters selected
and annotated by Sarah
Greenough, *Georgia O'Keeffe:
Art and Letters*, p. 184.
To Waldo Frank, summer 1926,
Lake George.
Washington, DC: National
Gallery of Art in association
with New York Graphic
Society Books, 1987.

Page 38: Jack Cowart and
Juan Hamilton, letters selected
and annotated by Sarah
Greenough, *Georgia O'Keeffe:
Art and Letters*, p. 231.
To Maria Chabot, November
1941, "In the Air."
Washington, DC: National
Gallery of Art in association
with New York Graphic
Society Books, 1987.

Page 39: Georgia O'Keeffe
Above the Clouds I,
1962/1963, oil on canvas
Gift of The Burnett Foundation
and The Georgia O'Keeffe
Foundation
1997.05.014/CR# 1474

Page 40: Jack Cowart and
Juan Hamilton, letters selected
and annotated by Sarah
Greenough, *Georgia O'Keeffe:*

Art and Letters, p. 224.
To Cady Wells, late
February 1938, New York.
Washington, DC: National
Gallery of Art in association
with New York Graphic
Society Books, 1987.

Page 41: Georgia O'Keeffe
Blue Black and Grey, 1960
Oil on canvas
Gift of The Burnett Foundation
2007.01.029/CR# 1440

Page 42: Tony Vaccaro
O'Keeffe at the Ranch, 1960
Gelatin silver print
© Tony Vaccaro
2007.03.010

Page 43: Georgia O'Keeffe,
Georgia O'Keeffe, p. 1.
New York: Viking Press, 1976.
© Juan Hamilton

Page 44: Three Stones
Personal tangible property
Gift of Juan and Anna
Marie Hamilton.
Photo by Malcolm Varon

Back cover: Georgia O'Keeffe
*Black Mesa Landscape, New
Mexico / Out Back of Marie's II*,
1930, Oil on canvas
mounted to board
Gift of The Burnett Foundation
1997.06.15/CR# 730

*Date not confirmed

The Museum is dedicated to the artistic legacy of
Georgia O'Keeffe, her life, American Modernism,
and public engagement.

Georgia O'Keeffe Museum

www.okeeffemuseum.org